Thinking of Nature

Written and Illustrated by Amy Mucci

Dedicated to my Mom and Dad.
Thank you for raising me to love and appreciate the natural world.
My favorite memories are with our family at the cabin.

From the waves of the sea to the trees of the land,
Nature is wonderful, precious, and grand.
Each mountain and valley, each star up above,
Are part of this world that we cherish and love.

This beautiful earth can amaze and astound you.
Think of the wonders of nature around you!

Think of a

Flower...

Do you think of the charm of a single red rose?
The fragrance of lilacs, a treat for the nose?
A field full of daisies? The buzzing of bees?
The delicate petals of blossoms in trees?
Colorful blooms make a stunning display!
A walk in a garden can brighten your day.

Think of a

Mountain...

Do you think of spectacular, snow-covered peaks?
Or hard, rocky edges and icy, cold creeks?
The vastness, the greatness, the still in the air?
The view from the top that's enchanting and rare?

The reflection of clouds on a crystal-clear lake?
There's thrill and adventure, each step that you take.

Think of the

Sky...

Do you think of the blue of a bright sunny day?
Or the smell of the rain when the clouds turn to gray?
The chill in the air right before the first snow?
Or the twinkling of stars with the moon's gentle glow?

The blaze of a sunset with birds flying by?
There's magic and miracles up in the sky.

Think of a

Forest...

Do you think of a birch tree, or maple, or pine?
Of soft mossy earth and the twists of a vine?
The singing of birds and the rustling of leaves?
The elegant branches that sway in the breeze?
A zigzagging path by a cool, bubbling stream?
A walk in the woods often feels like a dream.

Think of the

Ocean...

Do you think of the waves as they ebb and they flow?
Or the corals and creatures that live down below?
The feel of the sand as you walk on the beach?
The way the horizon is just out of reach?
The sights and the sounds of the beautiful sea
Can make you feel peaceful, delighted, and free.

Reflecting on nature will open your heart,
And all of this thinking can now be the start.

Go out and explore! What do you see?
Notice each blossom, each insect, each tree.

Hear the songs of the birds. Feel the wind on your skin.

Sense the wonders around you and breathe it all in.

Be mindful and brave with your arms open wide
As you learn and discover the joys of outside.

Discussion Questions:

- How does being in nature make you feel?
- What words would you use to describe nature?
- Share a favorite memory being outside.
- If you could go anywhere in the world to experience nature, where would you go?
- What can you do to take care of and protect nature?

We experience nature through our senses. When you are outside, take time to be mindful and think about what you see, hear, smell, taste, and feel!

Visit www.brightwishbooks.com for fun activity ideas and worksheets.

Also by Amy Mucci: The Magic of Words (2021)

ISBN: 978-1-7377277-3-6 (hardcover edition)

ISBN: 978-1-7377277-4-3 (paperback edition)

ISBN: 978-1-7377277-5-0 (ebook)

Library of Congress Control Number: 2022913298

First Edition 2022

Written and Illustrated by Amy Mucci

Edited by Tamara Rittershaus www.picturebooktamara.com

Edited by Chelsea Tornetto

Formatted by Misty Black Media

Bright Wish Books

Rochester, NY

www.brightwishbooks.com

Made in the USA
Las Vegas, NV
12 December 2022

62131217R00019